a special DOOR

» **Ken Ham**

illustrated by
Bill Looney

First printing: October 2016

Master Books®, P.O. Box 726, Green Forest, AR 72638

Master Books® is a division of the New Leaf Publishing Group, Inc.

ISBN: 978-0-89051-977-6
Library of Congress Number: 2016951274

Unless otherwise noted, Scripture quotations are from the New King James Version of the Bible.

Printed in China

Please visit our website for other great titles:
www.masterbooks.com

For information regarding author interviews,

please contact the publicity department at (870) 438-5288.

Master Books®
A Division of New Leaf Publishing Group
www.masterbooks.com